THE ULTIMATE P~~~
LEAGI

150 QUESTIONS TO KNOW

By

HARRY RYAN

Copyright © 2017

Introduction

Welcome to The Ultimate Premier League Quiz.

Since its formation in 1992, the English Premier League has taken the world by storm. The unprecedented popularity has been driven by the excitement of the league.

There is no other sports league in the world that can boast the number of viewers that the Premier League can. It is broadcast in 212 territories to 643 million television screens. Estimates suggest there are 4.7 billion people worldwide who enjoy the spectacle.

I have been an avid football fan since the late eighties so remember the transition from the old 'Division 1'. At the time, there was no indication on the impact that the new structure would have on the game. From finances to some of the finest players from all over the world, the league was never the same again.

There have been some amazing moments on the pitch and off it, and the questions throughout the book reflect the most significant moments as well as some slightly more obscure events. Collating these moments have brought back some wonderful memories and I hope it provides the same enjoyment to you.

Harry Ryan.

TABLE OF CONTENTS

Introduction

Table of Contents

Chapter 1. Managers

Chapter 2. Goalkeepers

Chapter 3. Goals

Chapter 4. Grounds

Chapter 5. Champions and Relegation

Chapter 6. Transfers

Chapter 7. Bumper General Quiz

Chapter 8. Answers

Chapter 1. Managers

1) At which stadium did Phil Brown, then of Hull City, deliver his infamous half-time team talk on the pitch?

2) Who was José Mourinho's first signing at Chelsea?

3) How many times has David Moyes won the prestigious LMA Manager of the year award?

4) How many games did Alan Shearer win for Newcastle after taking over as manager in 2009?

5) Who was the first Italian manager to win the Premier League?

6) Who has managed Liverpool, Southampton, Blackburn and Newcastle?

7) Who managed Manchester City when they won their first Premier League title?

8) Who has managed Reading, Swansea and Liverpool?

9) Which Dutch club did Southampton manager Ronald Koeman leave in 2014 before joining the south-coast club?

10) Which club did Glenn Hoddle join after being sacked as England manager in 1999?

11) Who was the first Premier League manager to be sacked?

12) How many times did Sir Alex Ferguson win the Premier League Manager of the Month award?

13) Who was the first English manager to win Premier League Manager of the Year award?

14) Arsène Wenger succeeded which permanent manager at Arsenal?

15) Who was the first manager to be victorious over José Mourinho in the Premier League?

16) Which nationality was the first non-British manager to manage West Ham in the Premier League?

17) Ron Atkinson last managed which club in the Premier League?

18) After beginning the 2012–13 season in very poor form, who did QPR sack on 23 November 2012?

19) Who was manager when Wolverhampton Wanderers were relegated in June 2012?

20) Who succeeded Harry Redknapp as Portsmouth manager in November 2004?

CHAPTER 2. GOALKEEPERS

1) Australian goalkeeper Mark Bosnich made 178 top flight appearances for Aston Villa, but in three seasons at Chelsea how many times did he play in the league?

2) Which goalkeeper has made most premiership appearances

3) Which goalkeeper's father had spells as manager of Everton and Norwich?

4) What nationality is former Arsenal stopper Manuel Almunia?

5) Which club did Chelsea loan Thibaut Courtois to?

6) Which Goal Keeper has played for Manchester City, Newcastle and Aston Villa?

7) Which player has played 12 Premier League games for two clubs and has two title medals?

8) Name the only goalkeeper to win Spurs 'Player of the Year' in the Premier League era?

9) Which goalkeeper scored with an 83-yard free kick past Ben Foster during the 2006-07 season?

10) Who was the first goalkeeper to score in the Premier League?

11) For which country did former Bolton Wanderers goalkeeper Ali Al-Habsi play?

12) John Lukic is best known for playing for Arsenal, but which other team did he play for in the Premier League?

13) Who was the only goalkeeper to save a penalty from Matt Le Tissier?

14) Which former Coventry goalkeeper signed for Chelsea in November 2006?

15) In the Birmingham derby of September 2002, which Aston Villa goalkeeper miscontrolled a throw in from Olaf Mellberg and conceded a goal?

16) In what year did Ed de Goey sign for Chelsea?

17) Which goalkeeper was signed for Leeds by Howard Wilkinson in the summer of 1996/97?

18) Which German-born goalkeeper played non-league, Premier League, and international football?

19) Who was goalkeeper for the Blackburn Rovers side that won the Premier League in 1995? Tim Flowers

20) Which goalkeeper did Newcastle sign from Reading in the summer of 1995?

Chapter 3. Goals

1) Who scored the first ever Premier League goal?

2) Which England player scored in 46 different Premier League games throughout his career - and didn't lose any of them?

3) Who is the only person born before 1960 to score a Premier League hat-trick?

4) Who is the Premier League's all-time leading goal scorer?

5) Which team lost two games by an eight-goal margin in 2009-10?

6) Which player holds the record for scoring the most goals in his debut Premier League season?

7) The highest scoring Premier League game finished 7-4. Which two teams played?

8) Manchester United hold the record for the biggest win but who was it against and what was the score line?

9) Which two players have scored over 100 Premier League goals without ever scoring a penalty?

10) Who scored the first Premier League hat trick?

11) Who has scored the fastest Premier League hat trick?

12) Who was the first ever winner of the Premier League's Golden Boot?

13) How many different seasons did Ryan Giggs score in?

14) Who was the first player to score for seven Premier League clubs?

15) Which club have scored the fewest goals in a season: Derby County

16) Who was the first player to open a Premier League campaign with an own goal?

17) Who was the first African player to score in the Premier League?

18) Who was the first player to reach 100 Premier League goals?

19) Who won the first Premier League goal of the season award?

20) Who scored the fastest Premier League goal?

Chapter 4. Grounds

1) What was the smallest stadium in the 2008-09 season with a capacity of just 20,224?

2) Which Premier League ground is at the highest altitude?

3) The highest ever Premier League attendance was at Old Trafford in March 2007, but who were Man Utd playing?

4) What was Southampton's old stadium called before they moved into St Mary's?

5) Where did Sunderland play up until 1997?

6) Where did Manchester City play their home games before moving to Eastlands in 2003?

7) What is the nickname of Manchester United's stadium?

8) Which English football team used to play their home games at Ayresome Park?

9) Where did Derby play up until 1997?

10) Which club played at Valley Parade?

11) What stadium was named after a famous snacks brand between 2002 and 2011?

12) Which former Premier League team played at the JJB Stadium?

13) In which stadium did David Beckham score his 'halfway line chip' back in 1996?

14) The most famous "Kop" is found on the ground of what renowned Premier League club located in the north-west of England?

15) If you were seated in the Bullens Road Stand, which ground would you be in?

16) Which former Premier League team played at Bloomfield Road?

17) Which former Premier League club played at Highfield Road?

18) Which team previously played at Vetch Field?

19) Which team plays at Turfmoor?

20) What is the home ground of Blackburn Rovers?

Chapter 5. Champions and Relegation

1) Who went down in 1996-97 after being deducted three points?

2) Which striker made the PFA Team of the Year in 2004-05 despite being relegated?

3) Which team embarrassingly recorded the fewest points ever in a Premier League season?

4) Who was the first outfield player to play every minute of the season for a Premier League title-winning side?

5) In what season did Arsenal's "Invincibles" go the whole season unbeaten?

6) Who won the first Premier League title?

7) How many seasons was Dougie Freedman relegated from the Premier League?

8) Which club conceded 100 goals on the way to being relegated in 1993/94?

9) What was the last year that 4 clubs were relegated from the Premier League?

10) The first three teams relegated from the Premier League were Middlesbrough, Nottingham Forest and which other club?

11) With how many games to spare did Arsenal guarantee the 2003/04 season?

12) When Blackburn won the league in 1994-95, Alan Shearer was their top scorer. But who was his sidekick up front?

13) In what year were Oldham relegated?

14) Which Arsenal captain retired after winning the double in 2001-02?

15) Bradford City survived the drop in 1999/2000 at the expense of which team?

16) In what year did Portsmouth gain promotion to the Premier League?

17) Which club were relegated in their first season in the Premier League in 1997/98?

18) Which title winners surname was made up entirely from Roman Numerals?

19) Who are the only team to have received a gold version of the Premier League trophy?

20) How many times did Alex Ferguson win the Premier League?

Chapter 6. Transfers

1) For what club did James Milner leave Newcastle in 2008?

2) What is the highest value transfer between English clubs?

3) Which player joined Bolton on a free from Paris Saint-Germain and went on to spend four-and-a-half years with the club?

4) Which club signed Thomas Gravesen from Everton in 2005?

5) Which Italian joined Middlesbrough for £7 million in 1996?

6) Ossie Ardiles signed what striker from Monaco for Tottenham 1994?

7) The signing of which two players landed their club with a record fine of £5.5 million?

8) Which Brazilian signed for QPR from Inter in 2012?

9) Which player did Alex Ferguson pay £7.4m for, despite admitting never having seen him play?

10) Which former European Footballer of the year did Chelsea sign in 1995?

11) Which club signed Champions League winner Finidi George in 2001?

12) Manchester United signed Andy Cole for £6m and which player?

13) Which World Cup winner signed for Birmingham in 2002?

14) What Coventry City midfielder did Liverpool sign in the summer of 2000?

15) From which club did Liverpool sign Paul Ince in 1997?

16) Which Ballon d'Or winner signed for Chelsea in 2006?

17) What Argentinian signed for Manchester United for £28m in 2001?

18) Which 20-year-old did Arsene Wenger sign on a free from Marseille in 2004?

19) With which club did Liverpool agree a £12m fee for Steve McManaman before he went on to join Real Madrid?

20) Which Argentinian signed for Leicester in 2014 and went on to be the clubs Player of the Season?

Chapter 7. Bumper General Quiz

1) Which Premier League winners father played rugby for Wales?

2) What year did the Premier League start?

3) Who was the first sponsor of the Premier League?

4) In what season did Roman Abramovich take over Chelsea?

5) Which player holds the record for the most goals in consecutive Premier League games?

6) Kevin Phillips won the Golden Boot in 1999/2000, who was the next English player to do so?

7) Which player holds the record for most consecutive Premier League appearances (310)?

8) What was significant about Mario Balotelli's only assist in the Premier League for Manchester city?

9) Who scored the first 'perfect hat trick' (left foot, right foot, and header) in the Premier League?

10) What player scored four goals in 12 minutes after coming on as a sub versus Nottingham Forest?

11) Which goalkeeper has the record of 138 clean sheets for the same Premier League team?

12) How many clubs have never been relegated from the Premier League?

13) True or False - The Premier League has the highest revenue of any football league?

14) Which club placed third with a negative goal difference in the first EPL?

15) Which two players have scored Premier League penalties with both feet?

16) Roy Keane received a five-match ban and £150,000 fine after deliberately injuring a player. Which player was it?

17) In September 2008, which player did John Hartson kick in the face during a training session?

18) How many teams were in the first ever Premier League?

19) The lowest attendance was 3,039 in 1993 when Everton played away to which club?

20) Which two non-English clubs have played in the Premier League?

21) How many times has the league been renamed?

22) Which faced his first sacking in six jobs while at Sunderland?

23) Which former Liverpool played international football across four decades (1989-2010)?

24) Which player scored a hat trick in each of the top four divisions in England, as well as in the League Cup, the FA Cup, and International football?

25) Which Swede had a clause in his contract banning him from travelling into space?

26) For what club did Paulo Di Canio play when he pushed referee Paul Alcock?

27) Which Hull City player did Alan Pardew shove his head into the face of in 2014?

28) In 2005, Newcastle's Lee Bowyer had an on-pitch scrap with which team mate?

29) Pedro Mendes put the ball behind the line for Tottenham vs Manchester United in 2005 but the goal wasn't given. Who was the goalkeeper?

30) Against which team did Wayne Rooney score his Premier League first goal?

Chapter 8. Answers

Answers: Managers

1) Etihad Stadium
2) Paulo Ferreira
3) Three
4) One
5) Carlo Ancelotti
6) Kenny Dalglish
7) Roberto Mancini
8) Brendan Rodgers
9) Feyenoord
10) Southampton
11) Ian Porterfield
12) Twenty seven
13) Harry Redknapp
14) Bruce Rioch
15) Kevin Keegan
16) Italian
17) Nottingham Forest
18) Mark Hughes
19) Terry Connor
20) Velimir Zajec

ANSWERS: GOALKEEPERS

1) Five
2) David James
3) Ian Walker
4) Spanish
5) Atletico Madrid
6) Shay Given
7) Richard Wright
8) Neil Sullivan
9) Paul Robinson
10) Peter Schmeichel
11) Oman
12) Leeds
13) Mark Crossley
14) Magnus Hedman
15) Peter Enckelman
16) 1997
17) Nigel Martyn
18) Maik Taylor
19) Tim Flowers
20) Shaka Hislop

Answers: Goals

1) Brian Deane
2) Darius Vassell
3) Gordon Strachan
4) Alan Shearer
5) Wigan Athletic
6) Kevin Phillips
7) Portsmouth and Reading
8) 9-0 vs Ipswich
9) Les Ferdinand and Emile Heskey
10) Eric Cantona
11) Sadio Mané
12) Teddy Sheringham
13) 21
14) Craig Bellamy
15) Derby County
16) Kyle Walker
17) Peter Ndlovu
18) Alan Shearer
19) Dalian Atkinson
20) Ledley King

Answers: Grounds

1) Fratton Park
2) West Brom
3) Blackburn
4) The Dell
5) Roker Park
6) Maine Road
7) The Theatre of Dreams
8) Middlesbrough
9) The Baseball Ground
10) Bradford City
11) The Walkers Stadium
12) Wigan Athletic
13) Selhurst Park
14) Liverpool
15) Goodison Park
16) Blackpool
17) Coventry City
18) Swansea City
19) Burnley
20) Ewood Park

ANSWERS: CHAMPIONS AND RELEGATION

1) Middlesbrough
2) Andy Johnson.
3) Derby County
4) Gary Pallister
5) 2003/04
6) Man United
7) 3
8) Swindon Town
9) 1994/95
10) Crystal Palace
11) 4
12) Chris Sutton
13) 1993/94
14) Tony Adams
15) Wimbledon
16) 2003/04
17) Barnsley
18) Vidic
19) Arsenal
20) 13

Answers: Transfers

1) Aston Villa
2) 50 Million - Fernando Torres
3) Jay Jay Okocha
4) Real Madrid
5) Fabrizio Ravanelli
6) Jurgen Klinsmann
7) Javier Mascherano and Carlos Tévez
8) Julio Cesar
9) Bebe
10) Ruud Gullit
11) Ipswich Town
12) Keith Gillespie
13) Christophe Dugarry
14) Gary McAllister
15) Inter Milan
16) Andriy Shevchenko
17) Juan Veron
18) Mathieu Flamini
19) Barcelona
20) Esteban Cambiasso

ANSWERS: BUMPER GENERAL QUIZ

1) Ryan Giggs
2) 1992
3) Carling
4) 2003/04
5) Jamie Vardy
6) Harry Kane
7) Brad Friedel
8) It was for Sergio Aguero's title-winning goal vs QPR
9) Jimmy Floyd Hasselbaink
10) Ole Gunnar Solskjaer
11) Petr Cech
12) Six
13) True
14) Norwich City
15) Bobby Zamora and Obafemi Martins
16) Alf-Inge Haaland
17) Eyal Berkovic
18) 22
19) Wimbledon
20) Swansea City and Cardiff City
21) Four
22) Martin O'Neill
23) Jari Litmanen
24) Robert Earnshaw
25) Stefan Schwarz
26) Sheffield Wednesday
27) David Meyler
28) Kieron Dyer

29) Roy Carroll
30) Arsenal

CAN I ASK A FAVOUR?

If you enjoyed this book, found it useful or otherwise then I'd really appreciate it if you would post a short review on Amazon. I do read all the reviews personally so that I can continually write what people are wanting.

Thanks for your support!

Harry Ryan

Printed in Great Britain
by Amazon